7 Questions Manifesto

Have You Ever Thought About
The Language Around Disability Before?

A Small Change in Language Could
Create a Big Shift in Thinking

By

Lorna Marsh

Dedication

Inspired by my nephews, nieces, and fellow change-makers—empowering futures by questioning norms around language and choice, one conversation at a time.

Foreword

Language has a profound impact on our understanding and experiences.

This manifesto explores the complex histories, cultural contexts, and empowering implications of disability terminology. Through this journey, you are invited to pause, reflect, and consider your own answers to seven pivotal questions.

Remember, no answer is wrong—each response reflects your unique perspective, choice, and experience. Your honesty is invaluable.

This exploration encourages thoughtful consideration of circumstances, situations, and personal choice, fostering empathy, self-awareness, and inclusive understanding.

Preface

Sarah Mitchell

I have known Lorna for sixteen years, ever since we worked together in a large adult social care department. I remain inspired, humbled, and challenged by Lorna, who always makes me think—hard—about my attitudes, values, and the role of social care in people's lives.

Lorna's work in *Seven Questions* challenges us all to think differently and, after forty years in health and social care, it has transformed how I believe we should commission services in the future. We need to engage with young people from an early age about their hopes and ambitions, how they want to live their lives, and how we can support them to achieve those ambitions— unlimited in our thinking.

Language possesses transformative power. This manifesto aims to:

1. Challenge stigmatising language, stereotypes, and biases.
2. Empower individuals with disabilities to reclaim their narratives.
3. Inspire inclusive practices, promoting genuine choice.

Together, let us create a world where disability is celebrated, individuals are in control, and diversity is valued.

Lorna's strength makes me stronger; her continual desire to achieve change for herself and others drives me to want to be more and do more. In supporting her to write *Seven Questions*, I know it will inspire others to do the same.

I salute you, Lorna.

Introduction

This manifesto offers both personal and professional reflections on living with a disability and navigating the care industry, whether as a recipient or provider of care services. It focuses on the language surrounding health and social care, highlighting the need to pay close attention to it.

Embark on this transformative journey with me. Within these pages, we will explore:

1. The impact of language on perceptions of disability.

2. Strategies for inclusive communication.

3. Personal stories of resilience, empowerment, and authentic choice.

4. Practical guidance for organisations and individuals.

Join me in shaping an inclusive future, one thought-provoking question at a time.

This manifesto is designed to take you on a journey that reveals how I arrived at the conclusions presented. It aims to encourage discussion, enhance choice, and open up opportunities for positive change in how disability is perceived by future generations.

My Journey

Allow me to introduce myself—I'm Lorna Marsh. I hold a dance degree with honours (I was the first woman in a powered wheelchair to earn a dance degree in the UK). While my school days were enjoyable, my career has been truly fulfilling. I worked as a dance teacher with people of all ages with autism and other impairments. I also contributed to developing accessible exam papers and worked with an organisation specialising in Direct Payments. Throughout my career, I have earned the respect of colleagues, clients, and communities, consistently feeling included, listened to, and valued.

When I was younger, I had a strong passion for the performing arts. Creative writing held great significance for me, serving as an outlet to process my thoughts and address issues I struggled to discuss with others. Writing allowed me to express myself freely, and I found that putting my thoughts on paper made them more relatable. Words have always been a profound source of comfort, and the creative process granted me permission to be genuinely honest. Once I had written about a particular subject, I felt a sense of resolution, as if I no longer needed to dwell on it. Through my performing career, I had the privilege of collaborating with remarkable individuals whom I deeply respect and cherish.

I have two loving parents and three sisters. Growing up, our home was filled with animals. Today, I'm blessed with two nephews, two nieces, and one goddaughter, as well as numerous friends with children of their own. My sisters and friends have given me the opportunity to be an auntie and godmother, which means the world to me.

The last piece of information about me, which I have purposely left until now: I am disabled. The order in which I have told you things is very intentional. I have Cerebral Palsy quadriplegia. I am a permanent powered wheelchair user and have severe dyslexia. I also have a twenty-four-hour Direct Payment package, which I was allocated at a very young age and will always need.

When my nephews and nieces were born, I realised I would need to find appropriate language to explain things in a way they could understand.

When they were younger, this meant providing only basic information, such as, "I'm in a wheelchair because my legs don't work." As they grew older, I shared more details, and their questions became increasingly complicated. I saw this as a positive sign.

I also viewed it as an opportunity to frame disability in the way I would like the world to perceive it. I realised this was valuable since they represent the next generation, and I seized the opportunity enthusiastically.

They knew I had a disability and that I used a special bed, a powered wheelchair, and other equipment. When they were younger, they thought all of it was the coolest collection of gadgets ever; in fact, they still do. I realised I could use the equipment to interact and play inclusive games, transforming it into something positive. This marked the beginning of a very strong relationship.

I also had an assistance dog for the first seven years of their lives, which greatly facilitated our connection, and we all deeply miss him.

When they were younger, they loved taking turns driving my powered wheelchair whenever they got the chance. To them, it was the ultimate adventure, and I was more than happy to let them have a go under careful supervision. These days, they no longer sit on my lap, but now that they're older, they can walk alongside me while driving the chair when I'm too tired after a long day out. It's a small but significant bonus of them growing up—what once was a game has become a genuine help.

I remember one day being with my goddaughter and her little brother when she was trying to learn to roller skate. We discovered that if she held onto the back of my chair, I could drive along, and she could skate without falling. In fact, they both could. We worked as a team to achieve a successful result—mission completed. For me, this is a perfect example of a moment that always makes me smile whenever I think about it.

When I visited one of my nephew's schools, I demonstrated my assistance dog's intelligence and how he enhanced my independence. I was unusually nervous, eager for my nephew to be proud of me. I rehearsed the presentation numerous times. Upon entering the classroom, my nephew immediately stood up and introduced me: "This is my auntie and her assistance dog." I had never felt such pride; his introduction filled me with a surge of satisfaction even before the presentation had begun.

Afterwards, I returned to his house, and we spent hours playing in the garden. He sat on my lap and drove my chair. Before Mum came home, he exclaimed, "I liked having you at school today, but playing with you in the garden was even better." Some moments are truly unforgettable.

Another memory is when we all went to Wales on our first family holiday. It was a beautiful, sunny day—very picturesque indeed. My assistance dog had some free time and chose to walk alongside my youngest niece. It was lovely to see. She always had a phenomenal connection with him; they all did. Yet, being so young, I was surprised at how much she understood about dogs. They loved each other, and this deep bond helped strengthen our connection, as we both cherished having him around.

When my nephews were about five, I confided in my sister, expressing my need to establish my own relationship with my nephews and nieces. I emphasised that I must spend time with them independently, accompanied by my PA (which is what I used to call them when I employed privately). Otherwise, how would they truly get to know me, and vice versa? How could we build our own rapport outside the larger family dynamic?

My sister understood and agreed, saying, "You need to do this your way. Figure it out, and we'll schedule a play date." So, we did.

I found myself trying to determine how to embody the aunt I envisioned, and I had the unsettling realisation that it would likely only be a version of my ideal. This was one of the few instances in my life when I felt angry about my circumstances, and I was taken aback by my own reaction.

The first play date remains unforgettable. We made milkshakes with various fruits, chocolate, and ingredients neatly arranged on the table. Everyone independently added ingredients to the NutriBullet, pressed down the container, and turned it on. Together, we counted down, transforming the experience into a mini factory. Everyone had a role, including me, helping with the countdown and judging the best milkshake flavour. This sparked a lively competition to create the ultimate milkshake.

That was the day I realised I could truly be an aunt, as they eagerly asked to return. I had successfully managed three wonderful hours with them, balancing responsibility and fun seamlessly. I cherish the countless memories we've built together—like when, in their younger years, two of them once stayed overnight, so reluctant to leave that it reaffirmed how much they enjoyed our time together.

I vividly remember one particular day when I was in the woods with one of my nephews. It was autumn, and leaves covered the ground. We chatted about everything under the sun when, out of the blue, he picked up a huge pile of leaves and playfully tossed them all over me! The unexpected surprise marked the beginning of a lively game. He chased me around the woods, repeatedly throwing leaves.

My PA at the time tried to intervene, understandably concerned about the muddy and unpleasant ground conditions. When my nephew was momentarily out of earshot, I discreetly reassured her, "Please don't worry; it's absolutely brilliant! He spontaneously initiated play without considering my wheelchair or potential struggles. That instinctive decision truly warmed my heart!"

To me, this moment served as definitive proof that he saw me simply as Lorna—a person with whom he could have genuine fun! It's impossible to express quite how much that meant to me.

It is thanks to my nephews and nieces that this manifesto has been written, as they have profoundly opened my eyes to the importance of language and identity. By sharing my personal story and professional insights, I aim to positively impact how disability is perceived and discussed, ultimately achieving my goal of creating a more inclusive and empowering future for generations to come.

Seven Questions

Let me begin by asking you seven questions, which I will revisit at various points throughout this manifesto to see if your answers remain the same:

Question One – What does your own identity mean to you?

Question Two – How important is your own space, whether physical, mental, or both?

Question Three – Do you wish to be respected as an individual?

Question Four – How have you, or how might you, manage any unwanted changes in your life?

Question Five – What is your understanding of political correctness and how it is being used or misused today?

Question Six – What does the word 'care' mean to you?

Question Seven – How much value do you place on your freedom of choice?

Answer these questions quickly, without overthinking them, as your first response is often the most honest. Every individual's answer will differ, but every answer is correct because everyone's life path is unique.

Now, let's consider each of these question areas in turn.

Question One

What Does Your Identity Mean to You?

Identity has evolved for me over the years. As a teenager, it meant being cool; in my twenties, it involved earning my degree, enjoying life, and forming relationships. Now, it is about truly understanding and accepting who I am.

This question has always been vital for me. I have three sisters, including my twin, who sadly passed away shortly after our birth. For years, I felt incomplete, as though a part of my identity was missing. I was genuinely confused about where I should fit in.

About 12 years ago, I joined the Lone Twin Network (LTN), and every meeting reignites my strength, understanding, and pride in who I am.

I feel proud of my twin; she contributed a significant part of my identity—a bond that endures. Once a twin, always a twin.

I invite you to reflect on the experiences, relationships, and moments that have shaped you, and consider how your identity has transformed over time. Embrace who you are today.

Question Two

How Important Is Your Own Space, Whether That Be Physical, Mental, or Both?

I love having my own space on both counts—perhaps a little too much. When I am with people, it needs to be the right people: those I trust, who I have known for a long time, and with whom I share history—something to hold onto.

Some individuals need constant company and do not wish to be alone. Others, like me, prefer a balance between social interaction and time alone. Then there are those for whom the choice is taken away.

For instance, many elderly people may not choose to be on their own, yet that is often the situation they find themselves in. Similarly, some people with disabilities might mentally desire solitude while, physically, it is not always an option. They may not require support to navigate life mentally, yet they might need extensive physical assistance. The frustration of this imbalance is strong, and it is often the only aspect that gets noticed.

Once someone enters your home or private space, it is no longer private. You do the polite "hello, how are you? Nice to meet you," and in no time at all, they've helped you on the loo. At that point, you're probably not even sure you've remembered their name correctly.

After fifteen years of employing support privately, I made the decision to use an agency. This was due to a very difficult experience—which I won't detail here, as this manifesto is about moving forward, not looking back. I already understood how agencies work, including both their good points and the less desirable aspects.

It was very hard to find an agency that could match the flexibility I enjoyed when employing privately, as agencies are burdened with red tape—which I fully understand. It is a business, and they are required to do things properly, safely, and legally.

The Care Quality Commission (CQC) is an organisation that gives people a voice—a place to turn if they feel things are not being done correctly, whether for an individual or an entire organisation. It is a service that is very much needed and valued, having prevented many issues from worsening or even occurring.

Care agencies and care homes are closely observed by the CQC and social services. This scrutiny has driven them to document everything meticulously to satisfy regulatory bodies. While I fully appreciate the necessity of this, it does come with its challenges.

Agency support today is far more flexible than it used to be, provided you have a live-in carer. However, the last call-out for day support in the evening remains at nine o'clock, which is hardly conducive to adult life.

That said, I have been very fortunate to have regular carers for the past two years—a remarkable achievement considering it is through an agency. When I employed privately, some people worked for me for more than ten years. I loved that stability, as it is incredibly disruptive when someone leaves; it takes a long time for a new carer to adapt to your life. While they are adjusting, your life slows to a crawl. For example, clothes need to be very easy to put on, the days seem endless, and yet somehow, nothing gets done!

I would like to see agencies continue to evolve, as they have already made significant changes—so why stop now? However, one aspect that still bothers me is the overwhelming amount of paperwork.

As a recipient of agency support, I find it feels like a complete invasion of privacy. Every detail of your daily life is recorded in a file and shared among carers, agency staff, and even office employees you will likely never meet. They know when you use the toilet, when you bathe, when you have been ill—everything. How is that right? How can the simple right to privacy be taken away just because you signed on the dotted line? Surely everyone is entitled to privacy, aren't they?

When researching different agencies, I often asked if I could write a detailed document outlining my support needs, which could then be shared with carers, social services, and the CQC if necessary. The answer was always a firm "no" because of rules and regulations. This made me feel as if I were under constant surveillance, with my privacy continually violated.

I would love to see agencies introduce an option where clients can sign a disclaimer allowing them to choose what information is shared and with whom. Perhaps a yearly report, written and approved by the individual, could replace the current system. This change would make me so much happier.

I understand the need for precautions in cases of diminished capacity. For example, someone with Alzheimer's might struggle to communicate, and important information could be missed if different carers rotate in and out. In such cases, I believe information should be shared with a designated family member or agreed-upon individual who can document changes and ensure proper care. This approach might preserve some element of privacy.

I realise that this might not entirely align with the rules and expectations of social services and the CQC, but surely there are other ways to balance everyone's needs while maintaining privacy. I do not know anyone who would appreciate having their daily bowel movements, meals, and activities documented and shared.

Ultimately, I believe this question is about protecting an individual's personal space and their right to privacy.

Question Three

Do You Wish to Be Respected as an Individual?

Each person is unique in their preferences, from small to big life choices. When it comes to running a home, I've never met anyone who doesn't have things they like done a certain way, even the little things. For example, I can't bear it when a placemat with a picture on it is placed the wrong way up on the table, or when the lights are left on!

In the same way, people have different preferences regarding how they wish to be assisted. Since my difficult experience that led me to transition to agency care, I know I do things very differently now. I used to have my PAs much more involved in my life—they really knew my family and friends. Whilst there is inevitably some overlap, I now try to keep my personal life and my arrangements as separate as possible. I make it clear to my carers: *I have chosen you to be my carer because I like you. However, these people are my family and friends, and I need you to remember that, because this is also my life as well as your job.*

I fully understand why society sees disability the way it does. I know it's because people are often relieved they are not in that situation, while at the same time wondering, *If I were, how would I cope?* That's normal—it would be odd if people didn't think that way. All I'm saying is that every disabled person has been on a journey of discovery. They know the answers to the questions you're wondering about. They've had plenty of time to work it out. They have found solutions, navigated access barriers, chosen the right agency, and organised their day-to-day assistance time and time again. The logistics of getting up every day never stop. In fact, working things out in every single area never stops. It is one big headache—a logistical nightmare! It can be complicated, expensive, and frustrating. That's what we need society to understand.

These are the cards we were dealt. What I'm asking for is an opportunity for every disabled person, whatever their story, to be seen how they want to be seen. We all have different preferences, but they are all valid. If you view someone only through the lens of their challenges, you risk keeping them stuck in the moment when their parents—or they themselves—first found out. They've moved on, so please move on with them. Join them on their journey to see how things can be improved for the next generation!

Personally, the inner able-bodied me is a country bumpkin, but the disabled me needs the city to reach my maximum independence! Different people, different needs. I've been recognising that more and more lately. It's hard to meet in the middle and be satisfied with the outcome because it's a constant compromise, and I was never as aware of that as I am these days. I don't really want to compromise anymore, so it's a relief when the compromise doesn't completely frustrate me. The two versions of me want to run away from each other—ironic, really, when you think about it! I have struggled for many years with my own limitations, as my mindset is fiercely independent, and the two sides of me aren't really friends with each other.

I believe Question Three is about respecting individual needs and preferences.

Question Four

How Have You, Or How Might You, Manage Any Unwanted Changes In Your Life?

Wishes and desires change naturally throughout life as we evolve as individuals. We are all just people with different life experiences that constantly shape our paths. It's exciting, in a way—new experiences, new passions, and new perspectives are created.

Adjusting to change can be difficult, though, as even positive life transitions tend to cause some stress. Over a lifetime, a person can expect to experience a significant amount of change. Some of these changes, such as marriage, childbirth, and new jobs, are generally positive, although they may come with their own unique stressors. Other major life transitions, such as moving to a new house, may also cause significant stress. These are all examples of typical life experiences.

But what happens when an event occurs in your life that is not good—something that alters your path beyond all recognition? Imagine there is nothing you can hold on to, nothing you recognise, not even yourself. Try, for a moment, to picture how you would feel and what you would need if it happened to you. What if you or a family member were to experience the onset of dementia? What if you or a loved one were injured in an accident and suddenly required care? What if you had a disabled child?

We can only begin to understand the trauma and enormous personal changes experienced in such circumstances. It is essential to remember this and treat people with the dignity and respect they deserve.

As you read this manifesto, I want you to think about how you would cope if the change you faced wasn't an average one. How would you manage if, overnight, everything in your life was different? What would you do if you suddenly needed care rotas and had strangers in your home while you were with your family? How would you feel if the people around you were all being paid to be there? Imagine wanting to visit your favourite venue—somewhere you've gone for years—only to find the steps now feel like an insurmountable mountain.

We need to keep in mind each individual's personal journey. What trauma have they experienced? When did it happen? What are they currently coping with? We can never truly walk in someone else's shoes; we can only stand by their side. Yet even standing beside them is still a slightly different path. Change isn't always expected, and neither is your reaction to it or the adjustments you may have to make.

It's crucial to respect the personal journey of each individual and be personable, responsive, and considerate in how we treat them.

I believe Question Four is about understanding the personal journey and the impact it has.

Question Five

What Is Your Understanding Of Political Correctness And How It Is Being Used/Mis-Used Today?

Political correctness, at its core, is about treating people with respect. It involves using language and behaviour that ensure everyone feels included, regardless of their background or identity. Choosing phrases like "person with a disability" or "person with a learning difficulty" acknowledges people's experiences while also recognising that they are more than just one aspect of their identity.

However, over time, the term has taken on a different meaning in public debate. Instead of simply being about inclusivity, "political correctness" is sometimes used as a criticism. Some argue that focusing too much on language can lead to censorship or self-censorship, making people hesitant to speak openly for fear of being labelled "too PC" or overly sensitive. When that happens, discussions can feel more restricted rather than more open.

There is also the risk of political correctness being used as a smokescreen. Some organisations are quick to adopt inclusive language and make public statements about diversity, but that does not always lead to real change. When the focus is more on appearing progressive than on tackling deeper structural issues, it creates the illusion of progress while inequalities remain unchallenged.

At its best, political correctness encourages respect and inclusivity, but when it is misunderstood or misused, it can sometimes do more harm than good. The key is finding a balance—using language that is considerate without shutting down honest conversations and ensuring that inclusivity goes beyond words, leading to real, meaningful change.

Question Six

What Does the Word 'Care' Mean to You?

For those experiencing sudden trauma that results in disability—whether mental, physical, or both—the word *care* can make an already overwhelming situation feel even more daunting. They are already adjusting to a life-altering change, and now they must invite a stranger into their home. It can feel like being reduced to a child in an adult's body, completely dependent on others. In that situation, what would *care* mean to you? Having someone help you isn't a luxury or a preference—it's a necessity.

Finding the Right Terminology

Carer

A person, including children and adults, who looks after a family member, partner, or friend who needs help due to illness, frailty, disability, mental health difficulties, or addiction, and who cannot cope without their support. Crucially, the care they provide is *unpaid*.

As stated in the White Paper, this distinction is vital—being a carer is not a job; it is a role undertaken out of necessity, duty, or love. Yet agencies continue to use the term to describe paid support staff. If *carer* is meant to denote an unpaid role, why is it being applied universally in professional contexts? If agencies use this wording in every scenario, even though it only truly applies in the unpaid context, doesn't that challenge the notion of free support?

Supporting

To hold up, carry, or prop up.

(*Not exactly an empowering term.*)

Personal Assistant

A secretary or administrative assistant working exclusively for one person. In the context of care support, a *personal assistant* is someone who provides one-to-one assistance, often employed privately through Direct Payments.

While this term is becoming more widely recognised in the care sector—and is also used in foster care for care leavers—it still doesn't fully capture the essence of what support should be.

Handicapped

This word is no longer used in England because it originates from *cap in hand*—a reference to begging.

Many outdated terms have been replaced because they send the wrong message. For example, *The Spastic Society* became *Scope* because *spastic* had become a playground insult. Although language has evolved, I still feel the current terminology around disability doesn't always empower.

One of my nephews once said, "People who are cared for are ill or in hospital after an operation. You're not cared for—you're not sick." His words resonated with me. Some of the language we use acts like a highlighter, drawing unwanted attention to a narrative we'd rather avoid.

Facilitation, Not Care

Reflecting on my own experiences, I've realised that I've never truly received *care* from my Direct Payment package. I don't need *care*—I never have. The support I need comes from friends and family.

It all depends on what the word *care* means to you. Has its portrayal distorted its meaning? Does it make older people feel as if they've failed? Has it taken on negative connotations? To me, it has become a word that triggers discomfort, frustration, and disappointment.

That's why I prefer to say I have *facilitation* from my *facilitator*.

A *facilitator* is someone who makes an action or process easier—helping individuals or groups achieve their objectives while remaining neutral. This term transforms the perception of support entirely. When I explain it to those assisting me, it shifts their understanding of what they're contributing.

I need *facilitation*—there's no doubt about that. It allows me to live life on my terms, giving me control over my choices and genuine independence. The word *care* suggests that the responsibility lies with the *carer*, but it should belong to the person receiving support. *I am facilitated, not cared for.*

Facilitation is a strong, clear, and affirming term. It doesn't require explanation—even if it isn't the most fluid word to say. Its meaning is exactly what I want the next generation to understand. The more young people grasp this concept, the more they can take ownership of their decisions and shape their own futures.

If you apply the word *facilitation* throughout this manifesto, it shifts the perception of disability. It allows others to see us not as people in need of protection, care, or support, but as individuals who require *facilitation* to be equals in society. Having a facilitator means owning your past, present, and future—including both the good and the bad decisions.

The Power of Language

Facilitation is more than just a word—it reflects a universal human experience. We all have dreams, desires, and diverse perspectives. Recognising this can change how we think and how we are perceived. I believe that *facilitation* could help Direct Payments reach their full potential by reinforcing autonomy, choice, and control.

Language evolves, and it's time we reconsider the words we use. People should have the freedom to choose terminology that best represents their circumstances—whether it's *facilitator*, *personal assistant*, *enabler*, or something else entirely. What matters is that they *own* their choice.

Care vs Facilitation

The key difference between *care* and *facilitation* lies in their focus.

- **Care** is about providing direct, hands-on emotional and physical support—offering comfort, stability, and security.

- **Facilitation**, on the other hand, is about empowering individuals—promoting independence, self-reliance, and personal growth.

As a physically disabled person, I rely on *facilitation* rather than traditional *care*. While *care* is essential for many, *facilitation* is what enables me to live fully on my own terms. My upbringing instilled a strong sense of self-sufficiency, a foundation that continues to guide my choices today.

I've observed that many people struggle to relinquish control, often clinging to a caregiving model that simply doesn't work for me. Instead, *facilitation* protects my autonomy, for me this is the very essence of adulthood.

Question Seven

How Much Value Do You Place on Your Freedom of Choice?

In my opinion, everyone has the capacity to make choices. The challenge lies in how we access the means to communicate with an individual to understand those choices. For example, we communicate with babies from a very young age, but we do so in a way that is understandable and accessible to them. They tell us when they like something and when they don't. They tell us when they're happy and when they're sad. They also tell us when they find something funny or when they're scared. This is all about communication and the sharing of information.

If a person has severe learning difficulties, they can still communicate and express their wishes. It might be in a different format or on a different level, but they are still communicating; they still have an opinion, and that opinion needs to be heard, seen and responded to. For example, an individual with learning difficulties might not be able to choose a cereal when faced with an entire cupboard full of options, as it can be overwhelming. But what if you take three packets out and ask which one they would like? You might get a definite answer that way. Everyone has preferences; we just might need to spend a little more time discovering what they are.

Do you have a food that you really can't stand? Mine is sprouts. Imagine if you were given them twice a week but were never asked if you liked them. You kept trying to express your dislike, but it left you feeling awkward and uncomfortable. You didn't know what to do. The frustration built up inside until one day, it exploded—you knocked all the food off the plate. You had never done this before, but you knew it would get a reaction. However, no one investigated why it happened, and the very next day, sprouts were on your plate again.

Without clear communication, frustration spirals out of control. One day, you reach a breaking point. Everyone needs to be heard, understood and respected. I believe we need to change the way we look at, think about and respond to things. It's not complicated or expensive; it is simply about opening the door to communication for all. No matter our personal circumstances, we all have a reason to communicate—something we want to say, something we need, or something we want.

When we learn a language, we take time to understand the words, phrases and correct pronunciation. It takes a long time, but it's worth it. When working with people who communicate differently, it is just as important to learn their language. If we don't take the time to do this, everyone misses out.

I believe everyone has the capacity to make choices, and all choices should be recognised and valued. What is important to one person may not be important to another, but that does not make it any less significant. This is especially crucial for those with learning difficulties, as communicating their preferences can be more challenging. The choices they express—no matter how small—must be fully understood, respected and acted upon to ensure their autonomy is upheld in every aspect of life.

Let's take away the opportunity for others to ask, "Does he take sugar?" Let's give control back to all the people mentioned in this manifesto and beyond. It's not about technology or making things complicated; it's about stripping it back and recognising how to communicate in a way that is clear, simple and direct. Every person who needs support has a past, a present and a future. The support they need is only one element of their life—one part of who they are. It is not the main element. In fact, it is the smallest.

My parents were incredible at enabling me to be who I was and focusing on what I could do, rather than what I couldn't. They accepted my limitations but then concentrated on possibilities, saying things like:

- "Okay, so you can't walk, but you can get a powered wheelchair."
- "Okay, so you're physically limited by your disability, but you can be facilitated."
- "Okay, so after this operation, you can't sleep in a normal bed anymore, but you can get a profiling bed."

They were always about making the best of a situation and finding a positive angle. I have always loved my parents, and as an adult, I truly appreciate just how phenomenal they were in setting up a framework that encouraged me never to give up. They approached challenges from different angles until a solution was found, and they made sure I was the one to find it. They also taught me that while limitations, pain and frustration are real, they should be acknowledged, dealt with and then let go. Honestly, they are incredible people, and I owe so much to them!

Direct Payments were created to offer greater independence and are available to everyone, no matter their disability. Originally, Direct Payments were not available for people with learning difficulties or mental health issues. Now they are, which is a significant and positive step forward. If someone needs help with any part of the process, they can be allocated a person to assist with the paperwork, ensuring equal opportunities.

I worked closely with the Department of Health when they were writing the white paper for the Care Act; it was a true privilege to be involved. I managed to secure more flexibility within the Direct Payments scheme. Originally, if someone moved to a new county, their Direct Payment would stop immediately, and responsibility for their care package would transfer to the new county. However, setting up a Direct Payment takes time. The longer someone has the package, the more beneficial it becomes. The Care Act now states that if someone moves house, they can retain their Direct Payment

31

for an extended period to allow them time to organise new arrangements. I believe this period is now three months. While this was not my original vision, it is a significant improvement on the previous system, where payments stopped immediately upon relocation.

What I originally wanted was for Direct Payments to function like a passport—something you take with you wherever you go. The package details would be recorded in the passport, outlining entitlements and ensuring it belonged to the individual rather than being tied to a postcode. This would create true flexibility and freedom of movement—just like everybody else has!

I believe *Question Seven* is about approaching each circumstance from different angles, investing time and effort in finding a way for individuals to take ownership of their life choices.

Seven Questions Revisited

Reflecting on the answers you initially gave to these seven questions, please consider whether your responses remain the same or if they have changed. Here are the seven questions again:

- **Question One:** What does your own identity mean to you?

- **Question Two:** How important is your own space, whether that be physically, mentally, or both?

- **Question Three:** Do you wish to be respected as an individual?

- **Question Four:** How have you, or how might you, manage any unwanted changes in your life?

- **Question Five:** What is your understanding of political correctness and how it is being used or misused today?

- **Question Six:** What does the word 'care' mean to you?

- **Question Seven:** How much value do you place on your freedom of choice?

Individual Story

Iwould like to tell you about an individual I had the opportunity to work with, as I feel this is a great example of developing communication and understanding.

When I met this individual and his family, he was about twenty-two years old. He had Down's syndrome and the mental capacity of a six-year-old. From the outset, his parents were determined that he would reach his full potential—wherever that bar ended up being. It was clear to me from our first meeting that they had worked incredibly hard to find ways to communicate with their son. I sat back and listened in awe at how they approached everything. I learned so much from them!

They knew that he learned in different ways but were determined to understand and relate to him. They said, *"He is our son; we needed to get to know him, just like anyone else would get to know their son."* They were committed to understanding his character, desires, passions, and wishes. They explained, *"We didn't know how we were going to do this yet, but we knew it would take us on a journey filled with new experiences. How can that be a bad thing?"* This truth-filled statement has stayed with me forever.

When they were told their son had Down's syndrome, they didn't know what to expect for the future. Now, they describe it as having gone on a journey with him—through being a stroppy toddler, a rebellious teenager, and a young adult wanting to live independently. With every step, his parents grew prouder of him. He has his own identity, his own wishes, and his own friends. His parents wanted to be part of his journey to independence and support him along the way.

We went on this journey of discovery together, and I loved every minute of it! We discovered that he wanted a red and yellow bedroom like Rupert the Bear and a National Rail duvet set. He wanted to be able to make his own sandwich—without the crust—do his own washing, and learn how to empty the vacuum cleaner so he could look after his own house like his mum does. He wanted to walk independently to his parents' house and the supermarket.

As a group, we didn't know whether this would be possible, but we were genuinely excited to find out! After a long period of planning, his Direct Payment package was worked out and agreed upon. A house was allocated, and several enablers (his preferred term) were found. Every step of the way, he had a very strong voice about what he wanted, which I applauded by listening. He also had no problem telling me when I misunderstood what he was trying to communicate. When he learned new things, it took him time to remember, but he always got there in the end.

I'm so pleased to say that, after years of repetition and perseverance, he has learned how to do all of the above completely independently! He is now a fantastically independent young man. He has a yellow vacuum cleaner and makes his own sandwiches with a special knife to cut the crusts off. He can change his own duvet without it ending up inside out—a skill that took a while to master.

He goes to the supermarket with a list of no more than four items so he can remember them. When he goes on his own, he always shops on the same day so he can see the same checkout lady. He tells her what change he needs back so he can recognise the money. She knows how to help him and does so with pleasure—they have a great relationship! Should she ever leave, it has been agreed with the supermarket that someone else will learn how to support him.

He also learned the journey to his parents' house with the support of his enablers, who had the patience for the repetition he needed. The last time I saw him, he was learning the way to a local drama group he had recently joined. I smiled and said, *"You'll have to find new wishes because you've achieved all the others."* We ended on a high-five.

If we had just focused on his disability and what he couldn't do, it would have been difficult to see what he *could* do. We all jump to conclusions—it's natural—but this is a manifesto that gives us the opportunity to reflect and change our behaviour.

A Testimonial

The testimonial you are about to read truly demonstrates that a small change in language can create a big shift in thinking—because it has!

I met Alicia years ago when we were studying for our performing arts degrees, and she later became my weekend facilitator. Sadly, we lost touch for some time. Nearly eight years ago, we reconnected on Facebook, only to discover that we now live near each other again!

This testimonial is about Alicia and her eldest son, Arrow. On my first reading, I was speechless and deeply moved. I had no idea what kind of journey they had faced in the time we hadn't been in contact or how much our initial conversations had really supported her.

Alicia is a phenomenal mum who will stop at nothing to help her son create the best opportunities for himself. Arrow is an incredible credit to both himself and his mum, and he is growing into an outstanding young man.

This testimonial is so honest; it shows that nothing is handed to you on a plate, but anything is possible depending on how you approach it. I hope their powerful example will demonstrate that facilitation is not just another passing concept. Instead, it represents a real opportunity for individuals to have genuine choice and control in their lives.

Testimonial

Alicia and Arrow Suarez-Garcia

My son, Arrow, was born on 21st March 2008. From the very beginning, it was evident that something was amiss, though it was unclear exactly what.

In the weeks and months that followed, Arrow would cry uncontrollably for long periods and needed to be held constantly. I couldn't put him down, nor could he settle for short naps in his cot. The moment he left my arms, he would wake. I quickly learned that the only thing that worked was carrying him in a sling all day.

You might think that crying isn't unusual—that all he needed was time to adjust to his new environment and the crying would eventually stop. Of course, I tried that, but Arrow's distress was on another level. He would scream continuously for hours until he fell asleep. It wasn't that he was struggling to adapt to a routine—it was as if, every time I put him down, it was a completely new experience, and he reacted with fear each time.

When weaning began, Arrow initially managed well with his first foods, but if anything touched the side of his mouth, he would start to cry, cough, and splutter until he vomited. I later realised that this cough was his way of reacting to anything he disliked, found uncomfortable, or struggled to tolerate. He would cough until he gagged, and then he would throw up.

Arrow showed little interest in climbing frames or playing with other children at baby groups. He walked on tiptoe everywhere, stiffening his hands as he moved. Art was not an option—paint sticking to his skin terrified him. What he did love, however, was carrying a screwdriver. In fact, he was fascinated by tools in general. His speech was unusually advanced, using descriptive words in perfect context, and he spoke both French and English with great ease.

At three and a half, we began an investigation at the child development hospital. As part of the process, Arrow had to attend nursery, where he would sit in his pushchair with his hands over his ears. At four, he was diagnosed with hypersensitive hearing, along with other undiagnosed sensory issues. This was a crucial piece of the puzzle. Until then, nursery staff had suspected he might be hard of hearing or even deaf, but the reality was the exact opposite.

I spent a lot of time watching him, observing his reactions to different sensory experiences, and wondering what his future would be like. Of course, to me, he was perfect just as he was.

Hoping to help him express himself, I joined the local library and read to him every night. Deep down, I wished that, in time, words would give him a way to describe what he felt. He loved being read to and had an astonishingly long attention span—sometimes I read to him for two or three hours at a time. This became our way of understanding each other. Since he loved words, we stuck with this method: I read, and he talked.

One day at the library, a father witnessed one of Arrow's worst meltdowns. Overwhelmed by the noise of other children, Arrow started throwing books at them in an attempt to make them stop. When I tried to intervene, he headbutted me, making my nose bleed. I had to carry him to a quiet corner, where he hit me, bit me, spat in my face, and began retching.

The father approached me and said, "You know, people like you really shouldn't be parents."

It was in that moment I realised the world had no understanding of our reality—and that it never would unless the gap in understanding was somehow bridged.

Lorna and I first met in 2002 at university while studying for our BA Honours degrees. Her weekend facilitator was on holiday, and she asked if I'd like to cover a shift.

"I'll talk you through everything you need to do," she assured me.

The weekend went well, and I became her regular weekend facilitator for the next three years.

This turned out to be one of the most significant friendships of my life. We spent countless days and nights talking. As I got to know her, I realised something extraordinary: although she had Cerebral Palsy and used a wheelchair, there were no limits to what she wanted—or could—do. She had an unstoppable drive, unshakable confidence, and to this day, the best work ethic of any person I have ever met, able-bodied or otherwise.

At the child development hospital, doctors refused to give Arrow a diagnosis. They said he was too young. They didn't want to "label" him. Some even implied the issue lay with my parenting. I soon realised that while the challenges were real, help was not forthcoming.

But I had learned something invaluable from Lorna. She had shown me that, with the right facilitation, a person could achieve anything. I began to apply that mindset to Arrow. If traditional support wasn't available, I would facilitate his needs myself, helping him find ways to navigate the world without limitation. I would think outside the box—just as Lorna had—so that Arrow could participate fully in life, despite what seemed to be a form of sensory processing disorder.

My goal was twofold: to facilitate his needs while ensuring acceptance. Without this balance, I feared he would be treated like something fragile, a problem to be "cared for" rather than a person to be supported in leading an independent life.

The word *care* might have suited him as a toddler, but how would he feel about it as a teenager trying to fit in? As a young man looking for a job? As an adult building a life of his own?

I knew that the way we framed his experience would shape his self-esteem and self-worth. If he saw himself as dependent, that would define his future. But if he understood that he had the power to facilitate his own life, he would grow up with confidence.

The perception in his own mind would outweigh the judgment of strangers—because he would be in the best position to educate others, just as Lorna had educated me. She taught me that the only true limitations were those we placed on ourselves. That sense of freedom was the greatest gift I could pass on to my son.

This understanding changed everything. It gave Arrow the freedom to develop confidence, self-esteem, and self-worth— without ever feeling like he needed to be cared for.

To our family, *facilitation* meant movement and possibility. *Care* felt restrictive and limiting. We believed that if facilitation became the standard approach, not only would it reframe adult mindsets, but children would feel more included in the world they were trying so hard to be part of.

One day, over coffee, I told Lorna everything. She listened carefully, then made a simple but powerful suggestion:

"If you want the meltdowns to subside, Arrow's boundaries need to be respected—whether they're socially acceptable or not. Facilitate his needs first, and the rest will follow."

She even had a solution for his discomfort with hugs.

"Carry a piece of ribbon," she suggested. "If he wants comfort or someone wants to show affection, he can hold one end of the ribbon while the other person holds the opposite end."

And so, we started finding ways to facilitate Arrow's integration into society while respecting his needs.

We continued working together to find solutions, though Arrow didn't always need my help. He had his own knife and fork, which we took everywhere. He used them even for foods like bananas, whose texture he disliked. To reduce his anxiety, we created a daily schedule on the wall, which I updated each evening for him to check in the morning.

Arrow attended mainstream school from the age of ten, after two years of home education. He made good friends, attended a samurai school for ninja training, and even won a junior filmmakers' competition for his short film *Bedroom Nightmares.* Though his facial expressions remained minimal, he learned to verbalise happiness and even taught himself to smile.

Through facilitation, Arrow has gained the confidence to set challenges for himself and overcome them. He owns his disability— not as a burden, but as something he can navigate with freedom.

And for that, I have Lorna to thank.

Alicia and Arrow update

The phone rings. A 17-year-old boy has landed at Gatwick Airport.

"Would you like me to come and meet you?" I ask.

"No, I'll see you at home. Bye."

The reply is short but confident. Beyond social norms that might deem it abrupt lies a deeper sense of pride and self-fulfilment—an assertion of newfound independence.

Arrow, who once clung to my apron strings, metaphorically speaking, is now a steadily independent young man. He continues to facilitate his own needs, wants, and aspirations, using language effectively to advocate for himself and his future. He has continued to try new things to discover his interests, has completed his GCSEs, and is currently doing a business studies apprenticeship in Malaysia.

Living abroad has brought both challenges and opportunities for growth, which he has embraced, setting his own boundaries within a framework that meets his individual needs.

Of course, some days are more difficult than others, particularly when unexpected (or even planned) events disrupt his routine. But Arrow has learned to navigate these moments, facilitating himself by applying strategies as needed and clearly voicing his requirements to those around him.

Facilitation, first introduced in childhood by the parent, gradually becomes a skill the child takes on for themselves. As they grow into adolescence and beyond, they learn to shape their own circumstances and implement the adjustments they need to live life to the fullest.

Final Reflections

Now, I ask you to reflect once more on the seven questions:

- **Question One** – What does your own identity mean to you?

- **Question Two** – How important is your own space, whether physically, mentally, or both?

- **Question Three** – Do you wish to be respected as an individual?

- **Question Four** – How have you managed, or how might you manage, any unwanted changes in your life?

- **Question Five** – What is your understanding of political correctness, and how is it being used or misused today?

- **Question Six** – What does the word 'care' mean to you?

- **Question Seven** – How much value do you place on your freedom of choice?

The care industry has progressed significantly; however, I believe it is time to take another big leap forward. If the seven questions in this manifesto were included, considered, and discussed within each individual's care file, it would shift the focus back to the person and enhance communication with them. It would ensure that individual identity and preferences are recognised and that life choices are maximised.

I would like to see a change in the details recorded in care plans and more consideration given to who needs access to them. For example, only the individual physically providing care—not everyone in the office—needs to know the frequency of toilet visits. Let's also move the legalities to the back and put a section on the seven questions upfront. Find out what matters to the individual, what outcomes they want to achieve in life, how they would like this to be facilitated, and the terminology they prefer. Ensure that, wherever possible, the individual makes their own life choices.

As you know, I believe the word *care* is passive, and my personal wish would be for it not to be used. However, if I were to ask for it to be deleted from the vocabulary of health and social care, I would be taking that choice away from others. The ultimate goal of this document is to give people genuine choice and control in their life's journey. *Seven Questions* is about getting the engine started— the rest is up to us all.

I have shared this *Seven Questions* manifesto with the belief that if I can help change the way disability is perceived today by changing the conversation around it, I can help make a difference for future generations.

My Pappy (Grandad) always loved the Frank Sinatra song *My Way*. Well, I like to think that this manifesto shows I introduced disability to the next generation *my way*! While writing this, my youngest niece was chatting to her mum one morning and said, *"Yes, I get it, because if you have a disability, you want to say what you need, and you want to still be treated as you."*

This made me so happy, as that's exactly how I believe disability should be seen. She summed it up in one sentence—where it took me a whole manifesto to do it!

If *Seven Questions* helps start a conversation, then positive change just might happen. It just might change things for the better.

One final question: **Do you agree?**

Personal Update

By October 2025, I will have lived in Hove for eight years, with the past three being particularly fulfilling.

I returned to privately employing facilitators—a decision driven by my desire to demonstrate resilience and growth. I wanted to prove to myself that I could overcome past challenges and succeed once more.

Recently, I pursued further education, achieving two significant milestones. I earned a distinction in a Diploma in Neurology—a passion since my teens—and completed a Foundation Course in Bereavement Counselling while volunteering with the charity that provided the course, supported by the National Counselling Society. This training has deepened my involvement with the charity for over a year, providing invaluable experience and knowledge.

Alongside *Seven Questions*, I have also written a novel called *Smooth Wheels*. This idea has been in my head since my early 20s, so it is truly special to finally put it down on paper. It has just been published, and I am both nervous and excited about it. *Smooth Wheels* follows the story of a talking wheelchair and its relationship with its owner, Top Hat Tom.

In October 2023, I took on the voluntary role of PR and Media Officer for the Lone Twin Network—a group for which I am immensely grateful and whom I have thankfully acknowledged at the beginning of this manifesto. This role provided a poignant opportunity to express my gratitude.

Shortly after starting, I received an email from Professor Nicholas Embleton, marking the beginning of a meaningful journey. I eagerly submitted a detailed description of the network and our interest in the Butterfly Project. Contributing to this initiative was deeply special, serving as a tribute to my twin. The swift response confirming our involvement was exhilarating, and the entire network was delighted.

For those unfamiliar with the Butterfly Project, there is a chapter following this update that explains its objectives and significance in greater detail.

Lorna Marsh

Butterfly Project
Professor Nick Embleton

I am delighted to contribute to this important book and share some of the work I have been involved in with lone twins and their families.

I work as a consultant neonatologist at the Royal Victoria Infirmary (RVI) in Newcastle upon Tyne, caring for sick newborn babies, many of whom are born prematurely. I completed my medical school education and paediatric training in Newcastle and chose to specialise in neonatology in the early 1990s. The challenges of looking after very small babies—some weighing less than 500 grammes—were initially daunting, but I was fortunate to have great teachers, both doctors and nurses, as well as parents who taught me invaluable lessons. Over time, I gained the technical skills, medical expertise, and communication abilities needed to care for premature infants and their families.

In the late 1990s, I completed a research MD focused on the nutritional requirements of preterm infants, trained in Vancouver, Canada, for a year, and returned to Newcastle as a consultant in 2002. A few years into my role, I had the opportunity to collaborate with sociologists and epidemiologists, leading us to conduct qualitative studies with bereaved parents. These conversations opened my eyes to the lifelong impact of baby loss and the emotional challenges families face, especially when one or more babies in a multiple pregnancy do not survive.

Starting in 2010, we undertook research with parents who had experienced twin or triplet pregnancies where at least one baby had died. Most often, these were premature births, but some families had lost a baby due to miscarriage or stillbirth. While parents were appreciative of the care provided by doctors and nurses, they often expressed sadness that little acknowledgement was given to the twin or triplet who had died. Some staff members were unaware that the surviving baby had been part of a multiple pregnancy, as this information was not always passed on during ward rounds or follow-up care.

Every bereaved parent we spoke to recalled someone—whether a staff member, friend, or family member—saying, *"At least you've still got one."* While often well-intentioned, this statement caused significant distress. It made us realise the need for better communication and support for families both in the neonatal unit and after discharge.

As a result, we ran a series of workshops with parents, during which a bereaved mother suggested using a butterfly symbol on the incubator or cot of the surviving baby. This simple yet powerful idea helped staff recognise and acknowledge the loss, ensuring that the baby's twin or triplet identity was not overlooked. Parents were also given the option to include the name of the baby who had died on the butterfly card. The Butterfly Project gained momentum, spreading to hospitals across the UK and eventually worldwide.

We published our research findings in medical journals, created a website for the project, and began working with the Skye High Foundation, established in honour of Millie Cann's twin baby, Skye, as well as *Footprints Baby Loss*, a charity that provides peer support for families who have experienced baby loss in multiple pregnancies.

In 2024, we launched a new research project, leading to a collaboration with Lorna and the Lone Twin Network. This ongoing study involves over 200 families and lone twins, aiming to deepen our understanding of their unique experiences. We hope to complete our analysis by 2025, using our findings to improve awareness, support, and education—not just for healthcare professionals but also for the public.

For more information about our work, please visit:

http://www.neonatalbutterflyproject.org

Nephew and Niece Adventures

Being an auntie remains a joy, although it's vastly different now that they're becoming their own people. I'm really enjoying watching their interests develop and their individual views evolve. Living in Hove means less frequent visits, but relocating provided invaluable independence—essential as a person with a disability. The countryside holds my heart, but Hove's accessibility is crucial. Tasks like visiting the doctor or bank are now effortless.

Since moving, I've grown comfortable with Hove's buses, which were previously inaccessible during my youth. My nephews and nieces visit during school holidays and have grown fond of Brighton and Hove themselves—maybe they'll relocate someday. Sharing activities remains vital; I still avoid being a spectator whenever I can. Playing Boccia together sparks competitiveness— a Marsh family trait! This inclusive sport brings us closer.

On 13 April 2024, I gifted my nephews an unforgettable birthday experience: descending the Brighton i360 from 450 feet via a rock climbing wire. The helpful staff adapted the experience with an incredible harness that kept me seated. Who'd have thought a 450-foot fall could be so comfortable? The boys were incredibly brave, genuinely relishing the day. We spent a sunny afternoon laughing, joking, and recounting our adventure.

I initially invited my brothers-in-law to participate, expecting an enthusiastic response. However, one revealed a previously unknown fear of heights. It's astonishing what you discover when proposing a 450-foot descent! My other brother-in-law agreed hastily but later admitted he hadn't fully grasped the details until the night before. His reaction was priceless—if the chair hadn't been behind him, I genuinely believe he'd have fallen to the floor. Watching the video, his repeated exclamations of *"It's high!"* were hilarious. Needless to say, next time I'll ensure thorough research precedes my invitations.

I hope the boys will always treasure the experience. They are still talking about it now, so that's a good sign. The view from that height was literally a bird's-eye view—utterly unique. Although the i360 closed in December 2024, Sarah Willingham from *Dragons' Den* signed the contract not long after to keep it open. I have no idea what opportunities will be presented, so I'm not sure whether my nieces would be interested.

One thing I do know is that I'm on a mission to find something we can do together that we will never forget. I'm looking forward to seeing what their next chapter holds and where their choices take them.

About the author

L orna Marsh has extensive personal and professional experience in social care, fostering a deep understanding of the field's complexities and nuances. She has delivered insightful talks on education and integration at Earls Court and numerous other venues, promoting inclusivity and empowerment.

Lorna's inspiring journey led to her serving as a torchbearer at the 2012 Paralympics. Additionally, she has presented the *Seven Questions* concept to several organisations, sharing valuable perspectives and expertise.

Lorna Marsh

Acknowledgements

Thank you to everyone involved in the first edition; without your efforts, the second edition would not have been possible.

I would also like to extend my gratitude to Nicholas Embleton for his valuable input in the second edition. It truly means a great deal to have the opportunity to promote the Butterfly Project.

www.ingramcontent.com/pod-product-compliance
Lightning Source LLC
Chambersburg PA
CBHW061718120626
46550CB00003B/1272